TIMES PAST
NORTH WALES

Top, Left To Right: **Climbers In Welsh National Dress On Snowdon, 1933; A farmer and his sheep on the mountains of Snowdonia, 1951; A Harbour Scene At Conwy, 1951.**
Bottom: **A Family Picnic On The Horseshoe Pass, 1936**

This book is part of the Times Past series, produced using photographs from the archives of the Hulton Picture Library including many from the famous Picture Post magazine.

Hilary Ellis

MYRIAD
LONDON

BANGOR AND MENAI

Separating the North Wales mainland and the Isle of Anglesey lies the Menai Strait, bridged in 1826 by Thomas Telford. The Menai Bridge was one of many challenges Telford faced in improving the London to Holyhead road, essential for crossings to Ireland. Boats to Anglesey set off from Bangor before the Menai Bridge was constructed. Today, Bangor is most famous for its university.

ABOVE: **MENAI BRIDGE, 1931.** The cables of the suspension bridge cast a shadow on the town of Menai Bridge. During the Victorian age, the small town developed as a popular resort on the coastal steamer route.

RIGHT: **MENAI STRAIT, 1950.** The Menai suspension bridge replaced a treacherous ferry journey from Bangor across the tidal Menai Strait. Many boats capsized or ran aground. In 1785, 54 people were swept away by a high tide after their boat became stranded on a sandbar.

ABOVE: **MENAI BRIDGE, LATE 1850S.** This extraordinary photograph was taken by the Victorian photographer Roger Fenton and shows the original wooden road surface of the bridge, replaced with a steel deck in 1893. Fenton, who is most famous for his photographs of the Crimean War, recorded many scenes in North Wales and several are included in this book.

RIGHT: **MENAI, 1940S.** A 100 foot clearance under the bridge meant that tall sailing ships could continue to travel along the Strait. Telford proposed a suspension bridge far larger than any previously built.

Above: **BRITANNIA ROCK**, *c1950*. Magnificent lions carved from Penmon limestone guard the entrance to Robert Stephenson's tubular bridge, completed in 1850 to carry trains across the Strait. A disastrous fire in 1970 led to the bridge's reconstruction to carry both trains and road traffic, and the lions now sit largely unseen to travellers below the road surface.

Right: **BANGOR, 1931**. The University of Wales at Bangor opened in 1884 in an old coaching inn with 10 members of staff and 58 students. In 1911, the university moved to the hillside overlooking Bangor.

Left: **BANGOR, 1931**. The city's population quadrupled in the early 19th century, and many hotels were built to accommodate the passengers who arrived by railway.

Below left: **BANGOR, *c1931***. Traders sell herring to a passer-by. For centuries great shoals of herring were caught off the west coast of Wales, but during the inter-war years the herring industry went into decline.

Above: **MENAI BRIDGE, 1939**. The iron cables of Menai Bridge are replaced by steel versions, as traffic continues across the bridge. Before their replacement, the chains could hold a weight limit of just 4.5 tons per vehicle, so overweight vehicles had to carry their load in two or more trips.

ANGLESEY

Populated since prehistoric times, the Isle of Anglesey (Ynys Môn in Welsh) came to be known during the middle ages as Mam Cymru "the mother of Wales", for its fertile fields. It has also been a fertile ground for the Welsh language. Edward I sought to intimidate the Welsh with his largest castle at Beaumaris, but most visitors to Anglesey stop only briefly on their way to Ireland.

ABOVE LEFT: **BEAUMARIS CASTLE, 1932.** Workmen repair the walls of the northern gatehouse, left unfinished by Edward I in 1298. Beaumaris was the last and largest of the castles built by the monarch to restrain the Welsh, and saw little action apart from during the Civil War in the 17th century.

ABOVE RIGHT: **BEAUMARIS CASTLE, 1857.** A man looks through the southern gatehouse to the inner ward and northern gatehouse of the castle. Designed by Edward's favourite architect, Master James of St George, Beaumaris is a true concentric castle and a mighty stronghold.

ABOVE: **BENLLECH BEACH, 1940S.** A child plays on the fine golden sands of Benllech bay, one of Anglesey's many beautiful beaches

LEFT: **CHURCH OF ST TYSILIO, 1968.** Beyond Telford's Menai Bridge lies Church Island and the tiny church of St Tysilio, founded in the seventh century by the monk, Tysilio.

ᴏᴠᴇ: **BEAUMARIS PIER, C1911.** Passengers board *La Marguerite* on their way back to ⸱ᴠerpool. Many thousands of tourists arrived in North Wales on paddle steamers until ⸱e decline of passenger services during the 1950s. *La Marguerite's* farewell voyage was ⸱eeted by schoolchildren at Menai Bridge in 1925.

ʜᴛ: **HOLYHEAD, 1934.**
⸱rries set sail for
⸱ublin from
⸱olyhead's inner
⸱rbour, protected
⸱om the rough Irish
⸱a by a one and a half
⸱le breakwater. In
⸱ctorian times, ferries
⸱ok up to seven hours
⸱ calm weather. Today
⸱e journey can be
⸱ne on high-speed
⸱perferries in just
⸱der an hour.

Lᴇꜰᴛ: **LLANFAIR PG, 1935.** A train arrives at the platform of the village with the longest name in Britain. Known as Llanfair PG to locals, the village name is believed to have been coined to attract tourists.

Aʙᴏᴠᴇ: **SOUTH STACK, 1938.** Postman RF Rees climbs more than 400 steps on his return from the South Stack Lighthouse. Situated on the extreme tip of Holy Island, west of Anglesey, the cliffs are the haunt of hundreds of noisy sea birds.

Conwy

The medieval walled town of Conwy sits on an estuary crossing and is dominated by Edward I's castle. Standing at the foot of Snowdonia, the castle was built as a key fortress in the king's fearsome "iron ring" to subdue the rebellious Welsh. A masterpiece of medieval military architecture, construction of the castle was completed within four years.

ABOVE: **CONWY ESTUARY, 1860S.** This dramatic estuary view shows Thomas Telford's Conwy Suspension Bridge alongside Robert Stephenson's tubular railway bridge. Both have mock fortifications at either end. The castle stands under an impressive Snowdonia skyline.

BELOW: **PENMAENMAWR HIGH STREET, 1950S.** Once on the main route from Conwy to Holyhead, Penmaenmawr is now bypassed by the busy A55. William Gladstone was a frequent visitor who often sang Penmaenmawr's praises.

ABOVE: **THE QUAY, 1951.** Tourists enter the fisherman's cottage, said to be the smallest house in Britain. Overlooking the quayside, this cramped home is just over 10ft (3m) tall and contains two rooms.

CONWY, 1936. A London, Midland
Scottish Railway train exits
...henson's tubular bridge, having
...ed through the castle grounds. The
...keeper's house stands to the right
...e narrow road bridge entrance.
...National Trust maintains the
...ge and toll house today.

PENMAENMAWR, 1932.
...struction workers build a road
...el as part of improvements to the
...ster to Holyhead road. The original
...e was narrow and subject to rocks
...g from great heights above.

LEFT: CONWY, 1957. A second road
bridge is added to cope with
increasing traffic congestion. In 1991
an immersed tube tunnel was
constructed underneath the estuary,
allowing traffic on its way to
Holyhead to bypass the town
completely.

BELOW: LANCASTER SQUARE, 1951. A
young man and woman sit at the foot
of Llywelyn's statue in the main
square of Conwy. Llywelyn the Great,
a heroic leader of Wales in the 13th
century, founded the Abbey of
Aberconwy where Conwy now stands.

LLANDUDNO AND GREAT ORME

Nestled between the two headlands of Great Orme and Little Orme, Llandudno is a planned town which was developed as a seaside resort on reclaimed marshland during the 19th century. Paddle steamers, and then trains, brought great crowds of visitors to the charming Victorian pier, long crescent promenade and sweeping sands.

RIGHT: **LLANDUDNO, 1860.** Rowing boats line the shore in front of the Promenade and the huge limestone headland of Great Orme. Before the pier was completed, visitors who arrived by boat were rowed to the shore and carried to dry land by local porters.

ABOVE LEFT: **MOSTYN STREET, LATE 1850s.** Mostyn Street began as dusty, unsurfaced road. Only later were shop windows and verandas added.

ABOVE RIGHT: **MOSTYN STREET, c1930.** North Western Gardens and Mostyn Street after some rain. The Mostyn family owns much of the land on which Llandudno has developed. Th family's vision ensured the town's development as the Victorian ideal of a respectabl seaside resort.

LEFT: **LLANDUDNO, 1939.** This fi aerial photograph shows the picturesque sweep of the bay and the grid system of town planning. To the far left of th bay, next to the Grand Hotel, stands the Pier Pavilion, Llandudno's main venue for shows and entertainment. A disastrous fire destroyed it completely in 1994.

ABOVE: **TY GWYN ROAD, 1940S.** The headland of the Great Orme is reached by Britain's only cable tramway, opened in 1902 to replace primitive roads. The site of an extensive Bronze Age copper mine, the Great Orme rises to over 650ft (200m).

ABOVE: **LLANDUDNO PIER, 1935.** Holidaymakers view "What the Butler saw" picture peep shows on the pier.

LEFT: **CAMERA HILL, 1930S.** A couple enjoy the view of Llandudno's pier from Camera Hill. The 2,200ft (700m) long pier was opened in 1876 as a port of entry as well as a site for recreational activity. A bandstand on the pierhead is now an amusement arcade.

Beach Towns

The Victorian preoccupation with fresh air and the health benefits of a stroll along the front led to the development of coastal resorts on the extensive beaches of the North Wales coastline. Each resort developed its own character, but the emphasis was on family holidays and entertainment.

ABOVE: **RHYL SANDS FROM THE PIER, 1890S.** Bathing machines can be se[en] on the beach: carriages that allowed a lady to change into a bathing dress and be drawn by horse to the shore. Rhyl was the earliest of th[e] North Wales resorts, with visitors arriving from the 1820s onwards. From 1848, the newly built railway brought well-to-do visitors and th[eir] servants, who often stayed for a month or more.

LEFT: **RHYL, 1939.** In the 20th century Rhyl became a popular destinati[on] for workers from the industrial towns of the midlands and north-we[st] England. Crowds flocked to the two-mile promenade which was extended in 1921.

RIGHT: **RHYL PAVILION, 1936.** An unusual photograph of the Rhyl Pavilion floodlit and reflected in the bathing pool. Opened in 1908 by Lord Mostyn, the roof was painted with camouflage paint during the Second World War. The Pavilion has now been replaced with a new building.

BELOW: **RHYL PROMENADE, C1929.** A big-headed policeman at Rhyl's annual carnival. After the development of the Marine Lake Pleasure Beach at the beginning of the 20th century, Rhyl became known as a centre for family fun and amusements.

RIGHT: **RHYL BEACH, 1939.** A curious toddler tries to get between two wicker deckchairs on the beach.

Above: COLWYN BAY, LATE 1950S. This aerial photograph shows the wide sweep of the bay with Rhyl in the far distance. Colwyn Bay's Victoria Pier stands in the centre of the bay with Rhôs-on-Sea pier to the left, demolished after storm damage in the 1950s. The white area shows the development site of the Elwy Road housing estate, whose houses were painted different pastel shades in the Welsh tradition.

Above: COLWYN BAY, 1890S. Towering over the beach is the luxury Colwyn Bay hotel, opened in 1871 with 92 bedrooms and a window for each day of the year. During the Second World War the hotel became the Ministry of Food's national headquarters, from where rationing for the whole of Britain was organised. In the 1970s the hotel was demolished when a buyer could not be found.

Left: PRESTATYN HOLIDAY CAMP, 1939. Demand for holidays and entertainment by the sea led to the construction of the Prestatyn Holiday Camp. The height of luxury, it contained furnished chalets, a ballroom, gymnasium, dining hall and lounges, swimming pools and sports facilities. Acquired by Pontins in the 1970s, it was demolished in the 1980s.

HOLYWELL AND THE VALE OF CLWYD

Inland from the coastal resorts of north Wales lie towns and villages rich in legend and scenic beauty. Holywell, a market town, has been a site of pilgrimage for centuries and came to be known as the "Lourdes of Wales". Further inland, delightful historic villages, towns and cities line the banks of the River Clwyd.

ABOVE: **BODELWYDDAN, 1880s.** Families picnic in front of St Margaret's Churc known as the Marble Church because of its white appearance and the 13 kinds of marble used in the interior. Consecrated in 1860, the church was erected by Lady Willoughby de Broke in memory of her late husband.

LEFT: **ST WINEFRIDE'S WELL AND CHAPEL, 1940s.** According to legend, Winefride spurned the advances of a local chieftain, who severed her head. spring rose from the ground where her head fell, and she was restored to li by her uncle, St Beuno. The spring is renowned for its healing powers and has been a site of pilgrimage for 1,300 years.

ABOVE AND RIGHT: **HOLYWELL, 1948.** In the early 20th century crowds of pilgrims flocked to the well on newly constructed railways, lured by tales of cures reported in the press each week. Pilgrims continue to visit the shrine, although numbers declined after the Second World War. A national pilgrimage is still held in June of each year. Many pilgrims pass three times through an inner bath, then pray kneeling on St Beuno's stone.

ABOVE: **ST ASAPH, 1900S.** A peaceful scene in the small city of St Asaph. The smallest ancient cathedral in Britain is seen in the background. It was built in Norman times and was destroyed four times – once by fire and three times by armies. The cathedral was restored in 1870 with many Victorian additions by Sir George Gilbert Scott.

BELOW: **RHUDDLAN, 1955.** The remains of Rhuddlan Castle stand beside the River Clwyd, crossed by the 16th century Rhuddlan Bridge. In Victorian times, the bridge was widened and iron railings were added. Because they were out of keeping with the original character of the bridge, the railings were replaced with walls of local stone when the bridge was further widened in the 1950s.

SNOWDONIA

The rugged ridges and summits of Snowdonia were known as Yr Eryri, "the abode of the eagles". Sailors travelling on ships from Ireland in the dark ages referred to the snow-covered peaks as Snowy Hills (or "Snaudune" in Gaelic) and Llewellyn the Great named himself "Lord of Snowdonia". The region is now a national park with the highest peaks in Britain south of the Scottish highlands. Yr Wydffa, its highest peak also known as Snowdon, is climbed by thousands of walkers each week.

RIGHT: **SNOWDON, LATE 1850S.** Victorian women accompany climbers on horseback on Snowdon's main summit path. Before the Snowdon Mountain Railway was completed, ponies carried the less active to the summit along the Llanberis path.

ABOVE LEFT: **SNOWDON SUMMIT, LATE 1850S.** The Ordnance Survey built a summit cairn in 1827, and in 1847 wooden huts were constructed around them. Two of these huts were hotels where visitors could stay the night. The modern-day summit building was designed by the architect Sir Clough Williams-Ellis and built in the 1930s.

ABOVE: **SNOWDON, 1950.** Members of the Ramblers' Association celebra[te] an Act of Parliament giving freedom of the mountains by climbing Snowdon's summit along the Miner's Track. A snowstorm threatens they make their way up the side of Llyn Llydaw – where Sir Bedivere reputed to have thrown Excalibur after Arthur's death. The lake is t[he] reputed home of the Lady in the Lake, who gave Arth[ur] the sword in the first place.

LEFT **LLANBERIS PASS, 1969.** The camping season gets under way at Pen-y-Pass, the highest starting point for hikes up to Snowdon's summit. The Snowdon Horseshoe cradles the scene, with the pointed peak of Y Lliwedd to the left, Crib Goch to the right and Snowdon hidden behind clouds between them.

BELOW: **TRYFAN, 1935.** A party of schoolboys rest on the Cannon, near the summit of Tryfan. A section of highway is seen 1,200ft (360m) below, where it skirts the margin of Llyn Ogwen.

SNOWDON MOUNTAIN RAILWAY, 1900S. A great triumph of Victorian engineering, the [S]nowdon Mountain Railway opened to passengers in 1896. The only rack and pinion railway in [Brit]ain, the journey from Llanberis to the summit is almost five miles long. After the passing [poin]t at Clogwyn there is a narrow and steep final climb, with incredible views of the slate [quar]ries at Dinorwig and the surrounding countryside north to Anglesey.

[BELO]W: LLANBERIS STATION, 1920S. The starting point of the Snowdon mountain railway is near to [Lly]n Padarn. The first part of the route up the mountain is over a viaduct with 14 arches before [star]ting the long haul up to the ridge and the mountain summit.

ABOVE: TRYFAN, 1953. Members of the British mountaineering party, who are planning to climb Mount Everest, test equipment on the rugged Tryfan. The lower slopes of Carnedd Dafydd are visible stretching into the background and dotted with sheep.

SHEARING TIME IN SNOWDONIA

The Snowdonia wilderness is home to many thousands of sheep, but goats and cattle were the chief source of income for medieval farmers. Hill farming still prospers, whereas the railway lines that once drove slate to the coasts are now scenic routes for tourists to enjoy the beauty of Snowdonia's more gentle valleys.

ABOVE: **FATHEW VALLEY, 1949.** A steam locomotive travels up the beautiful valley of the Afon Fathew on its way to Dolgoch, on the narrow-gauge Talyllyn railway. The seven and a quarter mile route opened in 1865 to transport slate, but after a serious rockfall in 1946 the traffic ended. Volunteers now maintain the route for unhurried passengers and rail enthusiasts.

BELOW: **TAN-Y-BWLCH STATION, 1870.** The Tan-y-bwlch station lies seven miles from Porthmadog on the Ffestiniog railway. The station originally had three loops to accommodate the long slate trains, and though today there are only two loops, it is still a major passing place for trains.

ABOVE: **BEDDGELERT, 1949.** In 1793, the landlord of the Royal Goat Inn created Gelert's Grave by the River Glaslyn to associate the village of Beddgelert with the legend of Llywelyn the Great and the faithful hound he mistakenly slew.

Above: **SNOWDONIA, 1951.** A farmer and his dogs, high up in Snowdonia, seek out sheep for shearing. The animals would be almost invisible against the rock in fleeces dark with the year's dirt and grease.

Left: **MERIONETHSHIRE, 1936.** From pastures in the mountains, the sheep are herded down to washing pools and shearing pens. These sheep await dipping in concrete baths five at a time. Their fleeces must dry for two days before shearing.

Below: **GLYDER FACH, 1930S.** Sheep are graded after inoculation against fluke and worm. Behind lie the twin lakes, Llynnau Mymbyr.

Above and right: **GWYNANT VALLEY, 1951.** The machine shears of the day would clip too close to the skin for the mountain climate so hand clippers were used. Sheep would be shorn with long cutting sweeps across the back – never lengthwise. The time taken over one sheep varied from two to six minutes according to skill, size of fleece and the temperament of the animal. Snowdonia farms would rely on a cooperative system of lent labour, clipping sheep after infrequent dry spells.

INDUSTRY IN SNOWDONIA

The scars of the slate industry can be seen throughout Snowdonia, but particularly around Blaenau Ffestiniog, the "slate capital of North Wales". More than 16,000 men once worked in often hazardous conditions quarrying slate, but today all that remains are disused quarries and mountains of waste. The scenic lakes of Snowdonia have provided water for Liverpool, and storage for hydroelectric power.

ABOVE: **BETWYS-Y-COED, 1855.** The Miner's Bridge still spans a gorge of rocks and loose stones over the Afon Llugwy a mile from Betws-y-Coed. It forms a steep ladder of fir-poles, which miners climbed on their way to work each day.

ABOVE RIGHT: **LLYN GWYNANT, 1949.** Tourists look across Llyn Gwynant and down Nant Gwynant, one of the Snowdon valleys.

RIGHT: **TRYWERYN VALLEY, 1957.** The fight for the deep-rooted hill farming community of Tryweryn Valley became a battle cry to prevent Welsh land from being flooded in order to supply Liverpool with water. The battle was lost, however, and a school, chapel, graveyard, village and six whole farms were eventually flooded.

ABOVE: **LLANBERIS, 1956.** Manchester University geography students plot the positions of soundings being taken by canoeists on Llyn Padarn to ascertain course for the 1958 Empire Games row events. The railway line leads to Llanbe slate quarry and was used only for the transport of slate.

LEFT: **LAKE VYRNWY, 19** The dam that created Lake Vyrnwy was completed in 1889, submerging the village Llanwddyn. The first large masonry dam in Britain, its pure water are transported to Liverpool by aqueduct In dry summers when the water level drops, ruins of the old town sometimes be seen.

ABOVE: **BLAENAU FFESTINIOG, 1946.** Blaenau Ffestiniog's history and industry are slate and have been for five centuries. Grey slag tips meet the sombre streets of the quarrymen's homes. Though there are open slate quarries, most of the slate lay deep and had to be drilled and blasted out.

RIGHT: **MINE WORKINGS, 1946.** Centuries of mining have robbed the mountains of their beauty, except for the grandeur of their outline.

ABOVE: **LLANBERIS, c1890.** After the blocks of slate had been sawn up, the splitting was done by hand, with a mallet and chisel. While the finishing was a more skilled job than the actual mining, the danger of silicosis, a lung disease caused by the dust, was smaller.

BELOW: **BALA HIGH STREET, 1920s.** At the eastern end of Llyn Tegid, Wales' largest natural lake, lies Bala, a Welsh-speaking community strung along a single high street.

ABOVE: **DESERTED VILLAGE, 1946.** Slate mining brought plenty of work to the mountains, too far for workers to go home every night. Miners lived high up in "barrack houses" during the working week and went home for Sundays.

LEFT: **CRAIG-DDU SLATE QUARRIES, 1934.** To save on long walks home down the mountain, workers return on specially constructed trolleys known as *car gwyllt*.

CAERNARFON

The site of Caernarfon, on a peninsula at the foot of the Menai Strait, has been an important military site for centuries. Before Edward I conceived Caernarfon castle in 1283, the Romans and Normans had constructed fortifications here. Edward's son, born in Caernarfon castle, became the first English Prince of Wales in 1301. In the 20th century, Edward VIII and Prince Charles became Princes of Wales in investiture ceremonies held in the castle.

ABOVE: **CAERNARFON**, *c*1940s. A dramatic view of Caernarfon's medieval town and the castle's polygonal towers joined by nine curtain walls. The castle's design is reminiscent of the Roman city of Constantinople. The famous Eagle Tower at the far right is crowned by a triple cluster of turrets. Stone eagles, now badly worn down, stand on the turrets as symbols of imperial power.

LEFT AND BELOW: **CAERNARFON**, 1911. Edward VIII was invested in the first of the modern investiture ceremonies 25 years before he ascended the throne and abdicated in December of the same year.

LEFT AND RIGHT: **CAERNARFON**, 1969. Four thousand guests watched the investiture ceremony of Prince Charles as Prince of Wales from the castle's ramparts. A television audience of 500 million viewers brought Caernarfon castle to worldwide fame, but the public investiture of an English prince infuriated Welsh nationalists.

ABOVE: **CAERNARFON, 1860s.** A tranquil scene in Caernarfon's harbour, where boats moor in the reflection of the magnificent castle.

LEFT: **CAERNARFON, 1930s.** Walkers stroll along the banks of the River Seiont. During the 19th century, after years of neglect, the castle ruins were sympathetically restored by the Victorian architect, Anthony Salvin.

BELOW: **CAERNARFON BAY, 1912.** The booming slate industry turned Caernarfon into a busy port in the 19th century. Paddle steamers regularly called at the port and were a vital link for passengers from Liverpool before the railway reached the town.

THE LLŶN PENINSULA

Wide bays and rocky coves lie between dramatic mountain cliffs on the beautiful Llŷn Peninsula. Iron Age hill forts, neolithic tombs and standing stones can be found on Llŷn. A popular site for sailing, holidaymakers are also attracted by the quiet beaches and unusually mild climate.

RIGHT: **PORTHMADOG, 1870.** The docks at Porthmadog were constructed in the early 19th century by William Alexander Madocks, after whom the town was named Port Madoc. Improved shipping and the development of the Ffestiniog railway meant that slate could be exported from the harbour to destinations such as Hamburg, Cadiz and South America. The harbour went into decline in the 1870s and is today a centre for tourism.

ABOVE AND BELOW: **CRICCIETH, 1924 AND 1913.** The Liberal statesman and prime minister David Lloyd George grew up near Criccieth and established his own law practice in the town, gaining a reputation as a solicitor willing to defend people against those in authority. Elected as a member of parliament at the age of 27, his famously fiery speeches gained huge audiences. Lloyd George supported women's rights during his time in opposition, but once in a position of power he did little to support the cause, and suffragettes responded by blowing up part of his Surrey home. Here, a suffragette has been attacked by the crowd at a meeting addressed by Lloyd George, and is escorted away by policemen.

ABOVE: **ABERSOCH HARBOUR, 1931.** Abersoch is known across North Wales for its yachting and sailing. The natural harbour and sandbanks stretch for two to three miles into Cardigan Bay.

LEFT: **LLANBEDROG, C1950.** A woman and child walk hand in hand down the steep rocky headland towards Llanbedrog beach. The beauty of the approach road and its sheltered sandy beach draws thousands of visitors each year.

RIGHT: **PORTMEIRION, 1960S.** Built by the architect Sir Clough Williams-Ellis between 1925 and 1975, Portmeirion is an Italianate coastal village of eclectic buildings, many salvaged from demolition sites. The Colonnade was originally built in Bristol around 1760 and, though damaged by bombs in the war, was rebuilt stone by stone in 1959. Behind it, the Chantry was designed by Williams-Ellis and built at the highest point in the village. Surrounded by sub-tropical gardens and woodland, Portmeirion is now a hotel and holiday village and has inspired guests and visitors such as Noel Coward, whose play *Blithe Spirit* was written here. The enigmatic Sixties television series *The Prisoner* was filmed here.

SOUTHERN SNOWDONIA

The best beaches in North Wales are to the west, where Tremadog Bay and Cardigan Bay touch the feet of Snowdonia. Harlech Castle and the Mawddach Estuary are passed by trains on the Cambrian Coast line as far as Barmouth, while the bulk of Cader Idris looms into view at just under three thousand feet.

RIGHT: **BARMOUTH, LATE 1850S.** Though today known for its tourism, Barmouth was a bustling port during the middle ages, known as Aber Mawddach, often shortened to Abermaw. This Victorian scene shows the harbour and oldest part of town, where attractive houses nestle on the steep streets and terraces of Dinas Oleu hill, the first property ever donated to the National Trust.

ABOVE: **BARMOUTH, *c*1920S.** Cader Idris in the distance stands behind the Mawddach Estuary as a steam train crosses Barmouth Bridge. More than 125 years old, the bridge is the only operational wooden viaduct in Wales.

LEFT: **DOLGELLAU, LATE 1850S.** A boy looks up at the wheel of a derelict mill near Dolgellau.

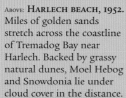

Above: **HARLECH BEACH, 1952.** Miles of golden sands stretch across the coastline of Tremadog Bay near Harlech. Backed by grassy natural dunes, Moel Hebog and Snowdonia lie under cloud cover in the distance.

Left: **MAWDDACH ESTUARY, c1920s.** The magnificent beauty of the Mawddach Estuary led Wordsworth to describe it as "sublime" and comparable to the finest in Scotland. Turner painted it, while Darwin wrote part of *The Descent of Man* in a house overlooking it. The estuary runs eight miles inland to Dolgellau and is the scene of spectacular sunsets.

Above: **HARLECH, 1890s.** Harlech castle, built by Edward I in the late 13th century, almost grows from the near-vertical cliff face on which it stands. Once the waters of Tremadog Bay may have lapped the foot of the castle; today the castle overlooks extensive sand dunes in a breathtaking location.

Left: **CADER IDRIS, 1949.** Five boys on a course at the Outward Bound School in Aberdyfi make their way up the mountainside. As a climax to a month's course of "character-forming" training, they must hike 30 miles over Cader Idris and back to the school.

ABERYSTWYTH AND ABERDYFI

Aberystwyth lies south of Snowdonia on Cardigan Bay, and is one of the largest towns of West Wales. It is home to the National Library of Wales and one of the colleges of the University of Wales. Two beaches are divided by a headland on which the ruined gatehouse of Edward I's Aberystwyth Castle stands.

ABOVE: **ABERYSTWYTH, 1900S.** Edwardian holidaymakers rest on the seafront. A wide promenade was constructed to protect the buildings from the ravages of the Irish Sea. To the right of the scene is the ruined Aberystwyth Castle. The castle was built by Edward I, but sadly its proximity to the sea meant that it rapidly decayed.

BELOW: **ABERYSTWYTH, 1922.** In 1872, the Old College Building was bought to establish the University College of Wales. The building was designed around an earlier mansion by John Nash as the luxury Castle Hotel of the railway age, but went bankrupt before completion. The mosaic represents Archimedes receiving the emblems of modern science and industry.

ABOVE: **ABERYSTWYTH, 1908.** Looking down Gr Darkgate Street, the town clock can be seen the top of Bridge Street. Built in 1856, it was taken down in 1956 as the top part had beco unsafe. Over the years many parts were lost b the 12ft pendulum still swings in the Ceredigion Museum. A new clock tower was completed in 2000.

ABERYSTWYTH, 1923. A fine view of
...rdigan Bay and the Irish Sea. The
...r was opened in 1865 and improved
...896 by the addition of the Royal
...r pavilion. Though the walkway is
...w significantly shortened due to
...eral storms, the Royal Pier is as
...pular as ever today. The harbour
...d marina can be seen to the left.

...T: ABERDYFI, 1895. In this
...otograph of Sea View Terrace and
...e harbour, fishing nets can be seen
...ing on the beach.

...w ABERDYFI, 1880s. Walking along
..."Roman Road". This route was
...ually built in 1808, and leads to
...nic Island and secluded coves.

...w RIGHT: ABERYSTWYTH, 1937. A group
...women take a raft out to sea on the
...ch at Aberystwyth.

Eisteddfodau

Poetry and singing predominate at the eisteddfodau in towns and villages throughout Wales each year. The National Eisteddfod has the greatest honours including the Bardic Crown and the Bardic Chair. Each year the National Eisteddfod moves to a new location, in North Wales one year and South Wales the next. The International Eisteddfod, however, has a permanent home in Llangollen and hosts international visitors each summer.

ABOVE: **LLANGOLLEN, 1952.** Since 1947, Llangollen has hosted the International Eisteddfod, bringing the nations together to compete in folk dancing and singing. In 1955, a young Luciano Pavarotti sang as a member of an Italian male voice choir. Here, participants perform in front of an eager crowd.

ABOVE AND BELOW: **LLANGOLLEN SCENES, 1950S** Bunting decorates the street as people from all over the world gather at the International Eisteddfod. The picturesque scenery of the River Dee and the rich history of the town has drawn visitors to Llangollen for centuries. An elegant bridge built by Bishop Trevor dates from 1345 and was widened in the 1960s to accommodate modern traffic.

LEFT: **MACHYNLLETH, 1937.** At the [tim]e, this was the smallest [to]wnship ever to have held the [Ei]steddfod. Locals came out to [wat]ch the ritual procession to [the] Gorsedd Circle, the chief [eve]nt of the National Eisteddfod.

[BEL]OW: **ABERYSTWYTH, 1916.** The [Go]rsedd procession carries [reg]alia through Aberystwyth [Ca]stle's grounds. The bardic [cir]cle of stones in the castle [gro]unds includes a stone to [rep]resent each of the 13 old [cou]nties of Wales.

[BEL]OW RIGHT: **MACHYNLLETH, 1937.** [An]na Davis and her attendants [in a] procession through [Ma]chynlleth. She represents the [fru]its of the earth and will [pre]sent the Archdruid with a [bas]ket of flowers "from the land [and] soil of Wales".

LEFT: **WELSH CHOIR, 1937.** Two white goats have been adopted as mascots by the Eryri Harp Choir of Beddgelert. The goats travel in the van used by the choir for carrying their instruments and national costumes.

RIGHT: **DENBIGH, 1939.** Two young women in national costume study the programme of the National Eisteddfod in Denbigh. The typical female costume was designed and made fashionable by Lady Llanofer in the mid 19th century.

Where North Wales meets England the landscape is flat but low valleys contain canals and rural communities.
Wrexham was the site of coal mining and iron works, but the River Dee separates the industrial areas from scenic
valleys. Llangollen is a dramatic entry point to Wales on the historic carriage route from London.

ABOVE LEFT: **WREXHAM HIGH STREET, 1900S.** Wrexham grew rapidly in the 19th century and this scene shows its hustle and bustle. At the end of the road lies the Old Town Hall which dates from the early 18th century. Used as a market on the ground floor and a town hall above, the building was demolished to widen the road in 1940.

ABOVE RIGHT: **MOUNT STREET, 1900S.** The famous steeple of St Giles' Church, completed in 1506, overlooks a scene on Mount Street, where the Nag's Head Inn stands to the left. The brewing industry helped to change Wrexham from a market town to an industrial area. Buildings from the old Soames' Brewery stand on Tuttle Street beside the inn.

ABOVE: **WYNNSTAY HALL ESTATE, 1920S.** Near Wrexham in the Dee Valley lies the former home of the powerful Williams Wynn family, built to a French style in the 19th century and with magnificent gardens landscaped by Capability Brown. The estate has recently been converted into luxury apartments.

RIGHT: **GRESFORD COLLIERY, 1934.** A crowd waits to hear news of miners entombed behind a raging fire in a mine at Gresford Colliery, near Wrexham. In total, 264 men lost their lives, including three members of the rescue teams, battling red hot coals and poisonous fumes. Gresford colliery finally closed in 1973 as coal mining in the area came to an end.

ABOVE: **DENBIGH, 1880S.** This view of Denbigh from the north-west shows the ruins of Edward I's 13th century castle overlooking the historic market town. The rocky hill on which the castle stands was the site of an earlier Welsh settlement. The well-preserved town walls attached to the castle ruins are almost two thirds of a mile long.

LEFT: **ROSSETT, 1940S.** The beautiful black and white timbered water mill of Rossett has appeared in many paintings and photographs. Standing on the banks of the River Alyn its four milling wheels produced flour for over 475 years.

BELOW: **NEAR BERWYN, 1934.** One-person boats known as coracles (from the Welsh *cwrwgl*) have been used across Britain since pre-Roman times. Capable of shooting the miniature rapids and needing only four inches of water to float them, these coracles were in use on the River Dee until the 1950s by local residents for fishing.

ABOVE: **LLANGOLLEN, 1930s.** A lone hiker stands on Velvet Hill and admires views of the River Dee.

BELOW: **A MERRY PICNIC, 1880s.** Welsh women enjoy a picnic in the countryside.

First published in 2009 by Myriad Books Limited
35 Bishopsthorpe Road, London SE26 4PA

Photographs copyright © Getty Images
Text copyright © Hilary Ellis

Hilary Ellis has asserted her right under the Copyright,
Designs and Patents Act 1998 to be identified as the
author of this work.

ISBN 1 84746 262 6
EAN 978 1 84746 262 6

Designed by Jerry Goldie Graphic Design
Printed in China

www.myriadbooks.com